LITTLE BOY STORIES FROM TIGER SCRUB

BY
STEPHEN GUEST

ILLUSTRATED BY TAMI BOYCE

Copyright © 2020 Stephen Guest
All rights reserved.

ISBN: 978-0-6488761-0-6

Cover and Interior Design by tamiboyce.com

To my mother and father
&
*My daughter Lauren
who was the first child in the whole,
wide world to hear about my adventures
in Tiger Scrub when I told them
to her as bedtime stories.*

ABOUT THE AUTHOR

Stephen Guest was born in south-west Queensland before he crossed the Great Divide to become a journalist, media adviser and screenplay writer. He won the Grand Jury Prize for the New York Screenplay Contest and was a finalist in the London Film Awards. When his mother had a health scare in 2019, he knew his time had come to write about his early childhood in Tiger Scrub as she was his last link to that remote and distant place which has since been reclaimed by the forests.

About the Illustrator

Tami Boyce is an American illustrator, producing works that combine a tone of whimsy, humour, and heart.

Tami says this about her work: "A love for drawing has been present in my life for as long as I can remember. I consider myself lucky to be able to incorporate what I love into what I do. I started creating art as a way to uplift folks and remind them to not take life too seriously. After looking at my work, I hope you see something that relates to you, touches your heart, or at least brings a smile to your face."

Table of Contents

Upside Down Rain	1
Chapter 1	1
Chapter 2	3
Chapter 3	7
The Fox, The Hens, and the Thunderbox	11
Chapter 1	11
Chapter 2	13
Chapter 3	17
A Greasy Little Pig Called Porky	19
Chapter 1	19
Chapter 2	25
Sausages in the Trees	27
Chapter 1	27
Chapter 2	31
Chapter 3	33

UPSIDE DOWN RAIN

Chapter 1

Years ago, in a faraway place that was hard to get to, a little boy named Stephen lived in a tiny town called Tiger Scrub. No-one knew why it was called Tiger Scrub because there were no tigers there, but everyone loved the name, especially Stephen.

GRRRR, Stephen would growl at the kangaroos and cows that hopped and MOOED around his house.

CAW, the crows would cry out as Stephen crept up on his hands and knees and pounced at them.

"Time to get up, sleepy head," Stephen's mummy said as she pulled back his blankets. "I've cooked scrambled eggs for you and boiled one for Frosty." Frosty was the family dog, a big black Labrador who was born one cold, wintery morning when thick, white frost covered the ground.

"Remember what's happening today?", Mummy asked.
Stephen opened one eye.

"They're starting work on the bore. We're going to have water, lots of it. We'll be able to have a big, long bath every night instead of using a bucket."

Stephen didn't know what a bore was, but he knew the big water tank was empty, and every week a truck would deliver drums of water for the 15 people who lived in Tiger Scrub where his mummy and daddy had a sawmill on the edge of a forest. Stephen knew everyone in Tiger Scrub, especially Mr and Mrs Pallisier, who had four children about his age. They were his playmates now, after Mummy had sent his three big sisters to board at a convent in the nearest town called Roma.

A big truck rumbled by outside — VROOM VROOM.

Mummy smiled. "The bore man's here."

Chapter 2

After breakfast Stephen walked towards Frosty's kennel with the hard-boiled egg but Frosty was nowhere to be seen. "Frosty, Frosty," Stephen called.

WOOF WOOF

Stephen looked through the palings of the house fence and saw Frosty following a man around in a nearby paddock. The man was holding two shiny bits of wire in his hands. "That's Mr Moffat," Mummy called through the kitchen window. "He's trying to find the best spot for the bore. Why don't you go and say hello to him?"

Stephen opened the gate and heard the ROAR of the sawmill. He saw Daddy pushing and pulling big pieces of timber, and Daddy waved to him. Frosty spotted Stephen as well, and bounded towards him. He ate the hard-boiled egg with one GULP and said thank-you with a big LICK.

Mr Moffat pointed the wire at Stephen. "I'm water divining," he said. "You know what that is?"

Stephen shook his head.

"If there's water under the ground, the wire will dip towards it. That's how I'll know where to put the bore. You want to help?"

Stephen nodded and Mr Moffat gave him the bits of wire. "Just cross one over the other and walk about. If you pass over water, you'll feel the wire fall to the ground."

Stephen held the two pieces of wire in front of him and started to walk. "That's the way," Mr Moffat said.

Stephen walked in a straight line and looked about. He couldn't see any water. He walked in a circle and buzzed like a bee — BUZZZ BUZZZ. He put the wire over his head and zigzagged like a fish — SWOOSH SWOOSH. Stephen thought he saw some water, but it disappeared when he walked towards it. Stephen clenched the wire in his teeth and imagined he was a propeller in a plane — BURRM BURRM.

"What are you doing?"

Stephen turned around and saw Gary, Johnny, Debbie and Dickie — the Pallisier children.

"Looking for water," Stephen said to Gary.

"There's some in the drum," Gary said.

"You look like a plane," said Johnny.

"Can we get in?" asked Debbie.

Dickie was too young to talk.

"Alright," Stephen said.

Stephen opened the door of the plane and they all piled in.

"Can I fly?" Gary asked.

Stephen will show you how to do it", Mr Moffat said. "He's really good at it."

And off they flew with Frosty following them.

BURMM BURMM

"Frosty's a cloud," Johnny said. "Let's fly into him and get wet."

Stephen pointed the plane towards Frosty and chased him about. Frosty barked with delight.

WOOF WOOF

"My turn," Gary said. "I'm next," said Johnny. "Me too," said Debbie.

And off they flew again.

After a while, when everyone had a turn, they all lay on the ground and had a rest. Mr Moffat looked at them and smiled. He got a white flag on a stick out of his truck and walked to the kids. He stuck the stick into the ground.

"This is where we'll dig," he said. "Best bit of divining I've ever seen."

The ROAR of the sawmill stopped, and Stephen's daddy walked towards them. It was lunchtime and Daddy had some sawdust in his hair from the logs.

"This sandy ground should be easy drilling," Mr Moffat said to Daddy. "I reckon we'll strike water by late afternoon."

Daddy looked pleased. "You kids had better get into the house yard," he said. "Drilling is dangerous business."

Chapter 3

Stephen, Gary, Johnny, Debbie and Dickie peered through the palings in the fence as Mr Moffat operated the big drill on the back of his truck.

THUMP CLANK THUMP CLANK THUMP CLANK

As dirt came out of the ground, Mr Moffat HAMMERED big steel pipes into the hole. After a few hours there was a big pile of dirt near the drill and the colour of the dirt was changing as the drill went deeper and deeper.

THUMP CLANK THUMP CLANK THUMP CLANK

"Won't be long now," Mr Moffat shouted.

Then all of a sudden, the drilling stopped, and Stephen heard a noise he had never heard before. A loud GURGLE, a big BURGLE, and BOOOMMMMMMM. Water GUSHED out of the pipe as quick as lightning and flew up into the sky. The water went so high it nearly reached the clouds. It was like upside down rain, and water droplets fell to the ground.

The sawmill stopped working and everyone clapped and cheered. "You kids can have an early bath if you like," Mummy said as she opened the gate.

Stephen, Gary, Johnny, Debbie and Dickie ran out of the yard and danced about in the rain.

They looked up to the sky and opened up their mouths and had a drink. It was warm and tasted a bit salty, but it was as clear as rain.

"Let's be a ship," Stephen said, as Gary, Johnny, Debbie and Dickie quickly got aboard.

BAAHH BAAHH, they all called out like a fog horn as they sailed around the bore, dodging whales and islands and coral reefs as water rushed up the pipe and turned the paddock into a big wild ocean.

WOOF WOOF, Frosty barked as he followed the ship about.

Tiger Scrub was never short of water again.

THE END

THE FOX, THE HENS, AND THE THUNDERBOX

Chapter 1

Stephen was the best egg collector in Tiger Scrub. Most days he would collect five or six eggs while Mummy watered and fed the fowls. A young hen named Henrietta was Stephen's favourite. Each morning Stephen would crouch down under a tin coop and pick the eggs out of a box that Daddy had made. Some days Henrietta was still sitting on her egg and Stephen would put his hand under her nice warm feathers. Henrietta didn't seem to mind and even let Stephen pat her. One day Stephen couldn't see Henrietta and called out to her, "Enywetta, Enywetta." Stephen couldn't pronounce Henrietta, but everyone liked Enywetta so much it became her name.

"I wonder where Enywetta could be," Mummy said as she joined the search among the turkeys and geese and ducks that shared the yard with the hens. Mummy looked towards the thunderbox, which was outside the chook pen. "What's that noise?" she said.

The thunderbox was an outdoor toilet about 15 yards from the house. It was a big pit in the ground and the toilet seat was a wooden bench with a hole in it. It had no running water, was dark and smelly and full of creepy-crawlies. Stephen never went there by himself as he was frightened of falling in and never being heard of again.

Mummy opened the thunderbox door and looked through the hole. "I don't believe it!" she exclaimed. There was Enywetta, sitting at the bottom of the pit, her feathers fluffed out like she was in a coop. "She must like the sawdust and bits of paper," Mummy said. Mummy used to sprinkle sawdust from the sawmill in the thunderbox every few days to keep the smell down.

Mummy got a rake and gently moved Enywetta. "CLUCK CLUCK," Enywetta plucked, a little bit annoyed. And there was an egg. Mummy scooped the egg up with the rake. "We'll have to give this egg an extra wash," Mummy said with a smile.

"Enywetta's a young, strong bird," Daddy said when he came home for lunch. "She can fly over the fowl-yard netting. We'll have to do something about that."

Chapter 2

The next morning Stephen and Mummy looked in the thunderbox and Enywetta wasn't there.

"Enywetta, Enywetta," Stephen called.

Stephen walked behind the thunderbox and saw a feather on the ground. Stephen was used to seeing feathers as chooks lose them all the time. Then he saw another, and another, and several more. They were Enywetta's.

Stephen started crying. "What's the matter?" Mummy asked. Then she saw the feathers and knew a fox had taken Enywetta.

"I'll teach that fox a lesson," Daddy said to Mummy at dinner. "I don't want him thinking he can get a meal here every night." Daddy got his shotgun and left it next to an open window in their bedroom. "A midnight surprise for that sneak," Daddy said as he put two shotgun cartridges on the window ledge.

When Mummy tucked Stephen into bed, she could tell he was still sad about Enywetta. "All chooks are lovely as

long as you are kind to them," Mummy said. "What about the grey-speckled one? She's nice and lays lots of eggs. Why don't we call her Juniper?"

"Ju ... Juni," Stephen said.

"That's it." Mummy smiled. "Tomorrow you can take Juni a bit of bread and butter and say hello to her." Mummy kissed Stephen, "Sweet dreams," she said.

"Juni," Stephen said.

Chapter 3

KABOOOMMMMMMMM

Stephen woke up in the mddle of the night as the house shook and rattled.

KABOOOMMMMMMMM

Stephen ran to his Mummy's bedroom and leapt into her arms as he saw Daddy standing next to the window with his shotgun.

The noise woke all the animals in the fowl yard.

The turkeys GOBBLED.

The ducks QUACKED.

The geese HONKED.

The hens CLUCKED.

And the crows that were perched in the nearby gum trees CAWED.

What a racket!" Mummy said. "We'll never get back to sleep."

Daddy stared into the pitch-black night and the fox was nowhere to be seen. "Neither will that fox," Daddy said with a smile.

. . .

The next morning, Stephen buttered a crust as he chewed on a bit of fried egg. "Juni will like that," Mummy said. "Get your basket and let's see how many eggs we've got today."

Stephen crouched down under the tin coop and saw Juni near a box. He held out the crust and Juni walked towards him. CLUCK CLUCK, Juni plucked as she pecked the crust.

Stephen looked up and saw Daddy with a big roll of netting. "This will keep Juni safe and stop the hens flying over the top," Daddy said.

The fox was never seen again.

THE END

A GREASY LITTLE PIG CALLED PORKY

Chapter 1

Stephen sat between his mummy and daddy as they drove to Roma, the nearest town to Tiger Scrub. They were on their way to pick up his sisters from the convent where they boarded, but this weekend was special. The convent was having a fete and a greasy-pig contest. "You better be careful when they let that pig go," Daddy said to Stephen. "Young boys can get a bit rough and they'll run right over you."

"His sisters will take care of him," Mummy said.

Stephen had never seen a greasy-pig contest before, but Rosie, Charmaine and Tracey had told him all about it. A little pig would be covered in something to make it slippery, they

said, and then it would be let loose in the crowd. Whoever caught the pig could take him home.

Stephen had seen lots of wild pigs running along the road and he knew they ran really fast.

He imagined catching Porky and putting him in the fowl yard with Juni. OINK OINK, Porky would say to Juni, CLUCK CLUCK, Juni would say to Porky as they ate their breakfast together.

Houses started to appear, and Stephen heard a marching band. "Here we are," Mummy said.

"Time for a toffee apple and a ride on the merry-go-round."

• • •

Stephen had never seen so many people. There were little kids and big kids and grown-ups.

They all walked and talked and ran and laughed and played games. Stephen soon forgot about Porky as he ate toffee apples and sucked on hard-boiled lollies. He played "Knock-em-down" and won a yellow balloon.

"Let's have a ride on the merry-go-round," his sister Rosie said. Charmaine put Stephen in a little boat with a steering wheel. "Hold on tight and wave to us," Tracey said. Stephen gripped the wheel as the boat spun round and round, higher and higher. And when he could see above the grown-ups, he saw a little pig in a cage behind a tent.

"Porky, Porky," Stephen called out. "Porky, Porky." Stephen pointed. When the ride was over, he led his sisters to the pig. "He come home," Stephen said.

"It's a she, not a he, and you'll have to catch her first," a big, tall man said. "Here, feed her this carrot while I get her ready for the greasy-pig contest." Stephen poked the carrot through the cage as the man got a bucket of thick, black grease from his truck. As Porky nibbled the carrot and OINKED at Stephen, the man put his hand into the cage and smeared grease over Porky's legs, her belly, her back and her tail. Porky changed colour from pink to black. "The grease will make her nice and slippery," the man said. "When people grab her, they won't be able to hold on."

The man got a wheat bag and put it over Porky and lifted her out of the cage. OINK, OINK, Porky protested through the bag. The man looked around at all the people. "Why don't you kids get on the back of my truck?" he suggested. "That way you'll be able to see where the pig goes when I let her out of the bag."

Chapter 2

Stephen, Rosie, Charmaine and Tracey stood on the back of the truck and heard a man over a loud-speaker announce, "Ladies and gentlemen, boys and girls, the greasy-pig contest is about to start." A huge ROAR went up from the crowd and people gathered from everywhere.

"The pig will be released in 10 seconds," the announcer said as he counted down, "10, 9, 8, 7, 6, 5, 4, 3, 2, 1."

Porky darted out of the bag as the crowd SHOUTED and moved towards her like a wave in a bathtub. They moved one way, then another. People rushed between two tents and around a car, around the merry-go-round and back again. People SQUEALED and YELLED as Porky OINKED and ran really, really fast.

Stephen saw one boy grab Porky by the leg, another by the tail and another by the head but Porky slipped away and kept on running. Two boys jumped at her together but somehow Porky wiggled her way out. By now Porky was nearly pink again.

"Porky, Porky," Stephen cried out as Porky ran straight past the truck and into a fence where Daddy was talking to another man. Daddy quickly pinned Porky against the fence, flipped her over, and grabbed her four legs. The crowd CLAPPED and CHEERED when they saw Daddy had caught the pig. "She come home," Stephen said as Daddy waved at him and his sisters.

∙ ∙ ∙

Later that night, when Mummy and Daddy pulled up at Tiger Scrub, there were four kids and one very tired little pig asleep in the car.

"What will we do with the pig?" Mummy wondered.

"They're smart and make good pets," Daddy said. "We might breed her as well."

Mummy and Daddy carried Stephen and his sisters into bed and Daddy put Porky in the fowl yard.

OINK OINK, Porky said as she looked around at her new home and had a drink of water.

CLUCK CLUCK, Juni replied.

THE END

SAUSAGES IN THE TREES

Chapter 1

It started to rain one day in Tiger Scrub when Stephen and Frosty were playing jump-the-broom — SPLATT. Stephen looked up to the sky as two big, fat drops of rain landed on his face — SPLATT SPLATT. Stephen opened his mouth and caught three — SPLATT SPLATT SPLATT.

And then it began to pour — SPLATT SPLATT SPLATT SPLATT SPLATT.

It rained all afternoon and all night. A big CLAP of thunder woke Stephen the next morning.

It kept raining and pouring, the old man's SNORING, Mummy began to sing. The sawmill stopped working, Juni stopped laying eggs, and creeks and rivers overflowed and turned the dirt roads into mudpies. The man on the radio said it was a flood. Tiger Scrub was cut off from the rest of the world. No-one could get in and no-one could get out — except the animals.

Emus, kangaroos and cows started to appear around the house with their joeys, calves and chicks. GRRRR, Stephen growled, but they were too wet and hungry to run away. Even Frosty stopped barking at them after a day or two and stayed in his nice, dry kennel. "The water's forcing the animals to higher ground to find food," Daddy said.

"Bit like us," Mummy said as she stirred a jug of powdered milk and poured it into a bowl of porridge for Stephen and Daddy.

"Googie," Stephen said. "Sorry, sweetie," Mummy said. "There'll be no eggs or sausages or toast until the sun comes out and we can drive into town."

Chapter 2

Stephen sucked on a hard ginger biscuit as he rocked his rocking horse and watched the rain tumble down from the veranda — ROCK SPLATT ROCK SPLATT ROCK SPLATT.

Something furry moved behind the fence. "Mummy, Mummy," Stephen yelled out.

"What?" Mummy called back from the kitchen.

Stephen couldn't speak as a koala climbed over the gate. Stephen ran inside and grabbed Mummy's skirt and pulled her out onto the veranda.

"I don't believe it!" Mummy said as the koala climbed up the stairs and sat in the corner. "If it's too wet for the koalas it's too wet for us. I'm going to arrange a food drop."

Stephen didn't know what a food drop was, but Mummy said if he looked up to the sky tomorrow a packet of hard-boiled lollies would fall out of a plane. Stephen stared at the sky all day and imagined catching one in his mouth like a drop of rain.

Chapter 3

The next day all the people from Tiger Scrub gathered on Mummy's veranda, with the koala sleeping peacefully in the corner. Stephen told Gary, Johnny, Debbie and Dickie all about the hard-boiled lollies, and they all opened up their mouths like he showed them to.

"I'll catch two," Gary said as he opened his mouth really wide.

"I'll catch three," Johnny said as he opened his mouth really, really wide with his fingers.

"Leave some for me and Dickie," Debbie cried out.

BBBBBBUUUUUURRRRRRMMMMMM

Everyone looked upwards and SHOUTED with joy as a little plane buzzed over Tiger Scrub.

"Get ready," Mummy said as the plane flew round and round and came lower and lower. The plane had a red nose with white wings and the pilot waved to them.

Everyone waved back, and then they began to CLAP and CHEER as food parcels fell to the ground like apples on a tree — THUD THUD THUD THUD THUD THUD. Cans of vegetables spilled out of one parcel, red apples splattered out of another, and a string of pink sausages got caught up in a tree like knotted-climbing rope.

"Let's get the food," Mummy said as the pilot waved goodbye and headed back to Roma. The men shooed away the kangaroos and emus and cows. Everyone walked out into the soggy paddock with wheat bags to collect the food.

Stephen found an apple under a clump of grass, Dickie found a can of carrots beside a tree stump, and Debbie shouted out, "Hard-boiled lollies!"

"You're such good helpers," Mummy said as they filled the wheat bags with food and headed back to the veranda. The women divided all the food among the families and Mummy gave Stephen, Gary, Johnny, Debbie and Dickie a lolly each.

A few days later the rain stopped, and the sun came out. All the kangaroos and emus and cows disappeared, and the koala woke up and climbed the nearest gum tree. Juni started laying eggs again and Mummy made a yummy breakfast of scrambled eggs and sausages and toast.

"Another googie?" Mummy asked Stephen.

"BBBBBBUUUUUURRRRRRMMMMMM," Stephen said.

Tiger Scrub was never short of food again.

THE END

www.ingramcontent.com/pod-product-compliance
Lightning Source LLC
Chambersburg PA
CBHW070312010526
44107CB00056B/2574